Cute Crochet Garden

Crochet Patterns for Plant Lovers

Copyright © 2023

All rights reserved.

DEDICATION

The author and publisher have provided this e-book to you for your personal use only. You may not make this e-book publicly available in any way. Copyright infringement is against the law. If you believe the copy of this e-book you are reading infringes on the author's copyright, please notify the publisher at: https://us.macmillan.com/piracy

Contents

Pull and Grow Amigurumi Plant 1

Sprouting Oddish.. 13

Snake Plant 19

Potted Baby Groot 35

Cactus in A Cup 53

Cute Crochet Garden

Pull and Grow Amigurumi Plant

Materials:

Lion Brand Yarn "Vanna's Choice" – Honey (A, 1 skein), Fern (C, 1 skein), and Kelly Green (D, 1 skein)

Loops & Threads "Charisma" – Espresso (B, 1 skein)

Crochet Hook, Size 3.5mm (US E/4)

Tapestry Needle

Cute Crochet Garden

Polyester fiber-fill

Wooden 1/8" dowel, cut to approximately 6" long

Black DMC Embroidery Floss (1 skein)

2 Black 1/2" buttons with shank

Embroidery Needle

Pink polyester felt

Craft glue

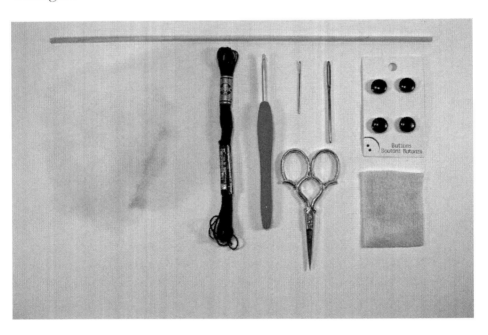

Cute Crochet Garden

Notes:

The pieces are all crocheted in the round in unjoined spirals (except Leaves). Use a locking stitch marker if necessary to mark the beginning of each round. When you complete a round, move the marker to the loop on your hook and continue crocheting.

Pattern:

Pot

With yarn A and E hook, make an adjustable ring, ch 1, sc 6 into ring. Pull tail gently to close ring.

Rnd 1: Work 2 sc into each st (12 sts)

Rnd 2: *(2 Sc into next st, sc into next st), rep from * to end of rnd (18 sts)

Rnd 3: *(2 Sc into next st, sc into next 2 sts), rep from * to end of rnd (24 sts)

Rnd 4: *(2 Sc into next st, sc into next 3 sts), rep from * to end of rnd (30 sts)

Rnd 5: *(2 Sc into next st, sc into next 4 sts), rep from * to end of rnd

Cute Crochet Garden

(36 sts)

Rnd 6: *(2 Sc into next st, sc into next 5 sts), rep from * to end of rnd (42 sts)

Rnd 7: Working in Back Loops Only (BLO) of each st, sc into each st (42 sts)

Rnds 8-9: Working into both loops, sc into each st (42 sts)

Rnd 10: 2 Sc into next st, sc into each st around (43 sts)

Rnds 11-12: Sc into each st around.

Rnd 13: 2 Sc into next st, sc into each st around (44 sts)

Rnds 14-15: Sc into each st around.

Rnd 16: Working in Front Loops Only (FLO) of each st, sc into next 21 st, 2 sc into next st, sc into next 22 sts (45 sts)

Rnds 17-18: Working into both loops, sc into each st (45 sts)

Rnd 19: Ch 1, turn, sc into BLO of each st around (45 sts)

Rnds 20-21: Working into both loops, sc into each st around (45 sts)

Fasten off, leaving a long tail for sewing. Fold down top edge of Pot along Rnd 19. Use tail to stitch down edge all the way around. Weave in ends.

Cute Crochet Garden

Dirt

With yarn B and E hook, ch 8, join to first ch with a sl st to make a ring.

Rnd 1: Sc 12 into ring (12 sts)

Rnd 2: *(2 Sc into next st, sc into next st), rep from * to end of rnd (18 sts)

Rnd 3: *(2 Sc into next st, sc into next 2 sts), rep from * to end of rnd (24 sts)

Rnd 4: *(2 Sc into next st, sc into next 3 sts), rep from * to end of rnd (30 sts)

Fasten off, leaving a long tail for sewing. Set Dirt aside.

Stem

With yarn C and E hook, make an adjustable ring, ch 1, and sc 6 into ring. Pull tail gently to close ring.

Rnds 1-14: Sc into each st around (6 sts)

Cute Crochet Garden

Rnd 15: 2 Sc into each st (12 sts)

Fasten off and leave a long tail. Insert the cut dowel into the Stem. Thread tapestry needle with yarn tail and weave into Rnd 14. Weave tail all the way around Rnd 14 and pull tightly to encapsulate the dowel inside the Stem. Knot the yarn tail to secure, and weave in the end.

Leaves

Make three or more leaves, using yarns C and D.

With C or D and E hook, ch 8.

Row 1: Work 2 dc into 3rd ch from the hook, dc into next ch, hdc into next 2 ch, sc into next ch, sl st into next ch.

Fasten off and leave a long tail for sewing.

Cute Crochet Garden

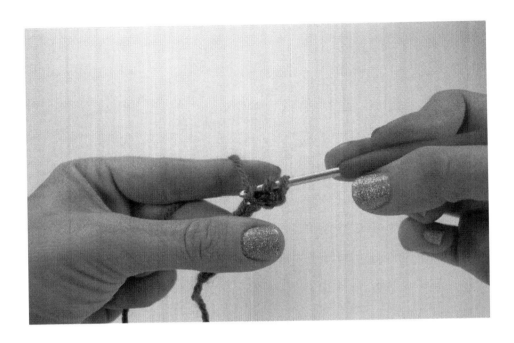

Assembly

Thread the tail from the Dirt piece onto your tapestry needle. Sew Dirt into Pot along unused back loops of Rnd 16, leaving a 2-3" opening. Insert polyester fiber-fill stuffing into the pot, small pieces at a time, filling in the outer area and leaving the middle of the pot less filled in. Insert the Stem from the inside of the hole in the center of the Dirt, out through the top. Push it down into the Pot, clearing a path through the stuffing so it will rise and lower easily. Finish closing the opening you left while sewing in the Dirt.

Cute Crochet Garden

Sew Leaves to the Stem using the yarn tails. Weave in the ends.

Thread the embroidery needle with embroidery floss, knotting one end. Insert the needle into the Pot between stitches, come up where you want your first "eye", through the yarn, and sew on a button, pulling the thread tightly. Pull up needle in the second eye location and sew on the second button. Insert needle back into the Pot's "face", and come back up at one side of the mouth. Make a "v" with the embroidery thread, keeping the stitches loose to round out the smile. Bring needle back up to the surface between stitches and knot the thread close to the fabric. Insert needle back into Pot and out through a stitch, clipping it close to the surface so that it retracts back inside.

Cut two 1/4" circles from pink felt and glue onto Pot.

Cute Crochet Garden

Abbreviations:

Ch: Chain

Sc: Single Crochet

Hdc: Half Double Crochet

Dc: Double Crochet

St: Stitch

Rnd: Round

Cute Crochet Garden

Rep: Repeat

Techniques:

Adjustable ring: Make a ring with yarn. Insert hook into ring, yarn over and draw up a loop. Ch 1, as directed in pattern. Work the stitches required in pattern into the ring. When complete gently, but firmly, pull tail to close up the ring.

BLO (Back Loops Only): Instead of inserting hook under both loops of the next stitch, insert hook under only the back loop of the stitch. This leaves an unworked loop in the front.

FLO (Front Loops Only): Instead of inserting hook under both loops of the next stitch, insert hook under only the front loop of the stitch. This leaves an unworked loop in the back.

Cute Crochet Garden

Sprouting Oddish

Materials:

4mm hook

Worsted weight yarn (size 4) in blue, green, black, and pink.

Polyester fiber fill

9mm safety eyes

Scissors

Darning needle

Cute Crochet Garden

Plant Pot will need to be 3.5" inches

Abbreviations: sc = single crochet

hdc = half double crochet

mr = magic ring

Sc inc = increase (2 sc in next stitch)

dec = decrease (sc 2 together)

ch = chain

dc = double crochet

Body (Begin in Blue)

Cute Crochet Garden

**It will be oval-shape initially, so you will have to stuff very firmly!

Pattern:

Begin with 6 sc in Magic Ring.

Round 1: inc around (12)

Round 2: *sc, inc* around (18)

Round 3: *sc 2, inc* around (24)

Round 4: *sc 3, inc* around (30)

Round 5: *sc 4, inc* around (36)

Round 6: *sc 5, inc* around (42)

Cute Crochet Garden

Round 7: *sc 6, inc* around (48)

Round 8-10: Sc around (48) (Place eyes in round 9, 9 stitches apart)

Round 11: *Sc 6, Dec* around (42)

Round 12: *Sc 5, Dec* around (36)

Round 13: *Sc 4, Dec* around (30)

Round 14: *Sc 3, Dec* around (24)

Round 15: *Sc 2, Dec* around (18)

Round 16: *Sc, Dec* around (12)

Cute Crochet Garden

Finish off and leave tail to close the hole.

Feet (Make 2)

Round 1: 6 Sc into Magic Ring (6)

Round 2: Sc around (6)

Finish off and leave tail for sewing

Leaves (Make 5)

Chain 6

Sl st into first stitch. Sc into next, HDC into next, DC into next two

Cute Crochet Garden

stitches, DC 6 times into the last stitch. It should be circled around by this point, now work on opposite side. DC into next 2 stitches, HDC into next, Sc into next, sl st into last.

The final steps now are to embroider the smile and blushing cheeks on!

Cute Crochet Garden

Snake Plant

Level: Intermediate

Finished Size: About 8" tall

Materials:

Worsted weight yarn (we used Sprightly Acrylic Worsted in Olive, Forest Green, Grass, Chocolate and Suede)

Size F (3.75mm) crochet hook

Cute Crochet Garden

Pair of 9mm black safety eyes

Small amount of embroidery floss and needle (for smile)

Polyester fiberfill stuffing

Tapestry needle

Stitch markers

Straight pins (optional, but super helpful when attaching the pieces)

Scissors

Cardboard (keeps your pot base flat)

Gauge

Gauge is not critical to this project. Just make sure the fabric you're making is on the tighter side with no holes, so your stuffing doesn't peek through.

Notes

The pot and dirt are crocheted in spirals; use a stitch marker to help keep track of where your rounds begin and end.

The leaves are worked flat in rows.

Cute Crochet Garden

The chain 1 at the end of the leaf rows does not count as a stitch.

Abbreviations

BLO – Back loop only

Ch – Chain

Dec – Decrease

FLO – Front loop only

Inv dec – Invisible decrease

Inc – Increase (work 2 sc into the same st)

Rnd – Round

Sc – Single crochet

Sl st – Slip stitch

St(s) – Stitch(es)

* – Repeat the directions in between * and * as many times as stated.

( ) – The number inside will indicate how many stitches you should have at the end of each round.

Good to Know: To spiff up on crochet abbreviations, here's a handy guide to all the ones you might see.

Cute Crochet Garden

Pattern:

Make the Pot

With Suade,

Rnd 1: 6 sc in magic ring. (6 sts)

Rnd 2: Inc in each st around. (12 sts)

Rnd 3: *Sc 1, inc* 6 times. (18 sts)

Rnd 4: *Inc, sc 2* 6 times. (24 sts)

Pro Tip: Pay attention to your increases in Rnd 4 and the remaining even rounds: they happen at the beginning of the round to create a more perfect circle.

Rnd 5: *Sc 3, inc* 6 times. (30 sts)

Cute Crochet Garden

Rnd 6: *Inc, sc 4* 6 times. (36 sts)

Rnd 7: *Sc 5, inc* 6 times. (42 sts)

Rnd 8: *Inc, sc 6* 6 times. (48 sts)

Rnd 9: *Sc 7, inc* 6 times. (54 sts)

Rnd 10: In BLO, sc 54.

Rnds 11 – 20: Sc 54.

Rnd 21: In FLO, sc 54.

Rnd 22: In BLO, sc 54.

Cute Crochet Garden

Fasten off and weave in the tail.

Add safety eyes between Rounds 14 and 15, leaving 5 sts between the eyes. Embroider a smile in between the eyes.

Cut a circle out of cardboard and place it in the bottom of the pot.

Make the Dirt

With Chocolate,

Rnd 1: 6 sc in magic ring. (6 sts)

Rnd 2: Inc in each st around. (12 sts)

Rnd 3: *Sc 1, inc* 6 times. (18 sts)

Cute Crochet Garden

Rnd 4: *Inc, sc 2* 6 times. (24 sts)

Rnd 5: *Sc 3, inc* 6 times. (30 sts)

Rnd 6: *Inc, sc 4* 6 times. (36 sts)

Rnd 7: *Sc 5, inc* 6 times. (42 sts)

Rnd 8: *Inc, sc 6* 6 times. (48 sts)

Rnd 9: *Sc 7, inc* 6 times. (54 sts)

Fasten off and leave a long tail for sewing. Set aside.

Make 3 Small Leaves

With Olive ch 2,

Cute Crochet Garden

Row 1: In 2nd ch from hook, inc. (2 sts) Ch 1 and turn.

Row 2: Inc in each across. (4 sts) Ch 1 and turn.

Row 3: Sc 4. Ch 1 and turn.

Row 4: Inc in 1st st, sc 2, inc in last st. (6 sts) Ch 1 and turn.

Row 5: Sc 6. Ch 1 and turn.

Row 6: Inc in 1st st, sc 4, inc in last st. (8 sts)

Change to Forest Green, ch 1 and turn.

Row 7: Sc 8.

Cute Crochet Garden

Change to Olive, ch 1 and turn.

Row 8: Sc 8. Ch 1 and turn.

Row 9: Sc 8.

Change to Forest Green, ch 1 and turn.

Row 10: Sc 8. Ch 1 and turn.

Row 11: Sc 8.

Change to Olive, ch 1 and turn.

Row 12: Sc 8.

Cute Crochet Garden

Change to Forest Green, ch 1 and turn.

Row 13: Sc 8.

Change to Olive, ch 1 and turn.

Row 14: Sc 8.

Change to Forest Green, ch 1 and turn.

Row 15: Sc 8. Ch 1 and turn.

Row 16: Sc 8.

Change to Olive, ch 1 and turn.

Rows 17 – 18: Sc 8. Ch 1 and turn.

Row 19: Dec in the 1st st, sc 4, dec in the last st. (6 sts) Ch 1 and turn.

Row 20: Sc 6.

Change to Grass and sc around the edges of the leaf, placing 2 sc in the tip. Do not sc around the bottom. Fasten off the Grass color and weave in tails. Leave a tail for sewing with the Olive yarn.

Cute Crochet Garden

Make 4 Medium Leaves

Use the pattern for the small leaf through Row 18 and continue with the directions below:

With Olive,

Row 19: Sc 8.

Change to Forest Green, ch 1 and turn.

Row 20: Sc 8.

Change to Olive, ch 1 and turn.

Row 21: Sc 8, ch 1 and turn.

Cute Crochet Garden

Row 22: Dec in the 1st st, sc 4, dec in the last st. (6 sts) Ch 1 and turn.

Row 23: Sc 6.

Change to Grass and sc around the edges of the leaf, placing 2 sc in the tip. Do not sc around the bottom. Fasten off the Grass color and weave in tails. Leave a tail for sewing with the olive yarn.

Make 3 Large Leaves

Follow the pattern for the medium leaf through Row 21 and continue with the directions below:

With Olive,

Row 22: Sc 8.

Change to Forest Green, ch 1 and turn.

Row 23: Sc 8.

Change to Olive, ch 1 and turn.

Row 24: Sc 8. Ch 1 and turn.

Row 25: Dec in the 1st st, sc 4, dec in the last st. (6 sts) Ch 1 and turn.

Row 26: Sc 6.

Change to Grass and sc around the edges of the leaf, placing 2 sc in the tip. Do not sc around the bottom. Fasten off the Grass color and weave in tails. Leave a tail for sewing with the Olive yarn.

Cute Crochet Garden

Attach the Leaves

Arrange the leaves on the dirt piece, placing 2 small ones in the front and staggering medium and large ones in different places behind. Leave one of each size for the back, placing the small one last. Remember to stagger them to help make it feel more natural. When you're happy with your placement, pin the leaves in place, then use the tails you left attached to each leaf to whipstitch them to your dirt.

Put It All Together

To create a clean edge, seam the pot through the unworked back loops from Round 21 to the last round of stitches of the dirt. Add fiberfill before closing the piece fully. Secure your tail inside the pot.

Cute Crochet Garden

Potted Baby Groot

Finished Size: Mine is approximately 7.5 inches tall.

Materials:

— H8/5.00mm and F5/3.5mm crochet hooks

Cute Crochet Garden

– Worsted weight yarn in Brown

– Sport weight yarn in Green

– Black embroidery thread or Black worsted weight yarn – If you'd rather not crochet tiny leaves, you can also use green felt to cut out leaves, and sew them on with green or brown thread.

– 2 9mm safey eyes (12mm looks cute, too!)

– small amount of Polyfil

– 1 12-inch pipe cleaner or some kind of wire for the arms

– scissors

– tapestry needle

– small plant pot

– a handful of small, smooth pebbles

– optional: fake moss, hot glue

Abbreviations in U.S. terms:

ch(s): chain(s)

sc: single crochet

Cute Crochet Garden

sk: skip

sl st: slip stitch

dec: decrease – you can use invisible decrease (invdec) or sc2tog

( ): work everything inside the parenthesis into the next stitch

[ ]: work everything inside the bracket the number of times indicated

Pattern:

Head Part A

With Brown and H hook, make magic ring, or ch 3 and sl st to 1st ch to form ring.

Rnd 1: Ch 1, 6 sc into ring. (6) Don't join rnds. Continue to work in a spiral.

Rnd 2: (2 sc) 6 times. (12)

Rnd 3: [(2 sc), 1 sc] 6 times. (18)

Rnd 4: [(2 sc), 2 sc] 6 times. (24)

Rnd 5: [(2 sc), 7 sc] 3 times. (27)

Rnds 6 -11: Sc evenly. (27)

Cute Crochet Garden

Sl st to next st to join.

You'll now work on his broken-wood head accents.

Rnd 12: You'll be crocheting triangular-ish and rectangular-ish shapes, and then slip stitching down one side of each shape to get your hook back to Rnd 11. We do this so we don't have to break off and re join over and over again to continue our work.

Ch 1, 3 sc evenly. Ch 1, turn. 3 sc evenly. Ch 1, turn. Sk 1 st, 2 sc evenly. Sl st down the side of the rows you just worked until you are about to work into Rnd 11 again.

4 sc evenly. Ch 1, turn. 4 sc evenly. Ch 1, turn. Sk 1 st, 1 sc, sk 1 st, 1 sc. Ch 1, turn. Sk 1 st, 1 sc. Ch 1, turn. Sl st down the side of the rows you just worked until you are about to work into Rnd 11 again.

4 sc evenly. Ch 1, turn. 4 sc evenly. Ch 1, turn. 3 sc, sk last st. Ch 1,

turn. 3 sc. Ch 1, turn. Sk 1, 1 sc. Sl st down the side of the rows you just worked until you are about to work into Rnd 11 again.

3 sc evenly. Ch 1, turn. 3 sc evenly. Ch1, turn. 1 sc, sk 1, sl st. Sl st down the side of the rows you just worked until you are about to work into Rnd 11 again.

4 sc evenly. Ch 1, turn. 4 sc evenly. Ch 1, turn. Sk 1 st, 1sc, sk 1 st, 1 sc. Ch 1, turn. Sk 1 st, 1 sc. Ch 1, turn. Sl st down the side of the rows you just worked until you are about to work into Rnd 11 again.

3 sc evenly. Ch 1, turn. 3 sc evenly. Ch1, turn. sk 1, 2 sc. Sl st down the side of the rows you just worked until you are about to work into Rnd 11 again.

3 sc evenly. Ch 1, turn. 1 sc , sk 1, 1 sc. Ch1, turn. Sk 1, 1 sc. Sl st down the side of the rows you just worked until you are about to work into Rnd 11 again.

Cute Crochet Garden

3 sc evenly. Ch 1, turn. 3 sc evenly. Ch1, turn. 1 sc, sk 1, sl st. Sl st down the side of the rows you just worked until you are about to work into Rnd 11 again.

Sl st into Rnd 11 and break off. Weave in end.

Insert eyes. You get to decide which part of the head should be the face.

Now you'll finish the top of the head. You're just making a circle to cover the hole.

Head Part B

With Brown, repeat Rnds 1-4 of Head Part A.

Sl st to next st to join. Break off leaving 24 inches of yarn.

Cute Crochet Garden

If you want a branch or two sticking out of his head, crochet these now and sew them to the top of Head Part B before you sew it to the top of Head Part A.

Branch

With Brown and H hook, ch 8, sk 1 ch, work 2 sl st evenly. Ch 4, sk 1 ch, work 3 sl st evenly, then continue to sl st evenly down original ch. Break off.

Short Branch

With Brown and H hook, ch 6, sk 1 ch, work 2 sl st evenly. Ch 3, sk 1 ch, work 2 sl st evenly, then continue to sl st evenly down original ch. Break off.

Lightly stuff Head Part A.

Cute Crochet Garden

Since Head Part B is 24 sts around and open hole of Head Part A is technically 27 sts around, you can't sew stitch for stitch, so just sew it on as best you can and make it look good. You can use Rnd 11 of Head Part A as a guide for sewing. While sewing, you also don't want the head to look like it has Frankenstein stitches going all around it, so try to sew as invisibly as you can. Put in more stuffing if needed.

Cute Crochet Garden

Body

Repeat Rnds 1-4 of Head Part A.

Rnd 5: [(2 sc), 3 sc] 6 times. (30)

Rnds 6-7: Sc evenly. (30)

Rnd 8: [dec, 3 sc] 6 times. (24)

Rnd 9: [dec, 2 sc] 6 times. (18)

Rnd 10: [dec, 4 sc] 3 times. (15)

Put in some stuffing or your sack of poly pellets. If you plan to wire the Body, anchor the bottom wire now if you like, but you can also run the wire after you complete the Body if you don't have a bag of pellets at the bottom.

Cute Crochet Garden

Rnd 11: [dec, 3 sc] 3 times. (12)

Rnds 12-13: Sc evenly. (12)

Rnd 14: [dec, 2 sc] 3 times. (9)

Rnds 15 – 25: Sc evenly, stuffing lightly as you go. (9)

Sl st to next st to join. Break off leaving 18 inches of yarn for sewing.

Sew top of Body to bottom of Head Part A. If you are wiring the body, trim the wire so that it reaches about half way into the head, and then poke the wire into the bottom of the head before sewing.

To prepare Arms, fold each end of the pipe cleaner to its center and then twist. If you are using wire, simply measure out the full length that you need for both arms.

Use a pointy stick to stab through top of Body where Arms will go. This will help guide the pipe cleaner arms through the body, but is not necessary for wire. Slide twisted pipe cleaner into place.

Cute Crochet Garden

You can now determine how long you want the arms and lengthen/shorten the pipe cleaner/wire accordingly. If you are using wire, bend the ends in now so that they are not so pokey.

Arms (make 2)

Pull out about 10 inches of Brown yarn for sewing later.

Cute Crochet Garden

With H hook, ch 3 and sl st to 1st ch to form ring. (Don't make a magic circle, or if you do, keep the opening loose because you need to fit the pipe cleaner through this hole.)

Rnd 1: Ch 1, work 4 sc into ring. (4)

Rnds 2 – 8: Sc evenly around. (4)

Slip Arm through pipe cleaner to see if it fits. Keep working evenly if you need more coverage.

When you reach the length that you need, create the finger branches.

Sl st to next st to join.

Ch 3, sk 1st ch, sl st 2 times. Sl st to next st.

Cute Crochet Garden

Ch 5, sk 1 st ch, sl st 4 times. Sl st to next st.

Ch 4, sk 1st ch, sl st 3 times. Sl st to next st.

Sl st to next st. Break off.

While weaving in your end, also sew through the base of the fingers to pull the fingers inward so they are not splayed too open.

Cute Crochet Garden

Leaves

The number of leaves and their placement are up to you!

With Green and F hook, ch 5 or ch 4 and sl st to 1st ch to form your leaf. Break off.

Tie leaf onto tree with yarn tails and then carefully weave in ends

Cute Crochet Garden

and/or hide them inside the tree.

Twisty Body Bits

If you want to add some twisty/viney bits to the body, simply work a length of chains about 12 – 18 inches for a shorter tree and 24 inches for a taller tree with Brown and H hook, then wrap chain lengths around Body, sewing down at each end, and also tacking down with a few stitches around the middle wherever you want to make sure the vine stays put.

Final Assembly

– Embroider a smile with black yarn or embroidery thread.

– Place baby Groot inside a small pot.

– Fill in with smooth pebbles to keep him upright. You might also need some pebbles underneath, so that he is not sitting too low in the pot.

– Decorate with fake moss.

– If you are giving this as a gift, and you don't want anything to move around, you can also hot glue your baby Groot to the bottom of your pot, or glue something to the bottom of the pot for him to stand on, and then glue him to that, then cover with pebbles, moss, or both!

Cute Crochet Garden

Cactus in A Cup

SIZE

6.5" tall (including the cup) using medium worsted weigh yarn size 4 and a 3.75 mm (F) crochet hook.

Cute Crochet Garden

You can adjust the size of your cactus by using thicker or thinner yarn and a different crochet hook.

Use the hook size that you find best to achieve a tight fabric so that the stuffing will not be visible.

ABBREVIATIONS AND SYMBOLS

mr: MAGIC RING: make single crochet stitches into an adjustable loo

sc: SINGLE CROCHET

ch: CHAIN

inc: INCREASE: make two single crochet in the same stitch

dec: DECREASE: make two stitches together

sl: SLIP STITCH

( ): REPEAT: repeat the pattern between the parentheses the number of times specified

[ ]: TOTAL STITCHES: number of total stitches in a round

Cute Crochet Garden

Materials:

Yarn (Colors: brown, green, pink, yellow)

Crochet hook: 3.75 mm (F)

Stuffing (polyfil, fiberfill, etc)

Small cup

Yarn needle

Scissors

Stitch marker (optional)

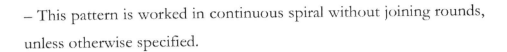

OTHER NOTES

– This pattern is worked in continuous spiral without joining rounds, unless otherwise specified.

– You can use a stitch marker or a piece of yarn to mark the beginning of a round so that you don't get lost.

Pattern:

SOIL

*work with brown yarn

1: sc6 into mr = [6]

2: (inc) 6 times = [12]

3: (sc1, inc) 6 times = [18]

Cute Crochet Garden

4: (sc2, inc) 6 times = [24]

5: sc in each stitch = [24]

6: (sc4, dec) 4 times = [20]

7: sc in each stitch = [20]

8: (sc3, dec) 4 times = [16]

9-12: sc in each stitch = [16]

13: (sc2, dec) 4 times = [12]

Stuff with polyfil firmly.

14: (dec) 6 times = [6]

Make a slip stitch, fasten off and weave in ends.

Make sure that it fits inside your cup! If it doesn't, you might try making it with a different size hook, or maybe changing to another cup or pot.

These are the 3 green parts of the cactus:

Cute Crochet Garden

LARGE PART

*work with green yarn

1: sc6 into mr = [6]

2: (inc) 6 times = [12]

Cute Crochet Garden

3: sc in each stitch = [12]

4: (sc1, inc) 6 times = [18]

5-6: sc in each stitch = [18]

7: (sc4, dec) 3 times = [15]

8: sc in each stitch = [15]

9: (sc3, dec) 3 times = [12]

10: sc in each stitch = [12]

Stuff with polyfil lightly.

Make a slip stitch, fasten off and leave a long tail for sewing.

Attach this part to the soil.

MEDIUM PART

*work with green yarn

1: sc6 into mr = [6]

2: (inc) 6 times = [12]

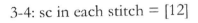

3-4: sc in each stitch = [12]

5: (sc2, dec) 3 times = [9]

6: sc in each stitch = [9]

Stuff with polyfil lightly.

Make a slip stitch, fasten off and leave a long tail for sewing.

Attach to the top.

Cute Crochet Garden

It doesn't have to be in the exact same position. You can change it up if you want!

SMALL PART

*work with green yarn

1: sc6 into mr = [6]

2: (sc1, inc) 3 times = [9]

Cute Crochet Garden

3: sc in each stitch = [9]

4: sc2, dec, sc3, dec = [7]

5: sc in each stitch = [7]

6: dec, sc5 = [6]

Stuff with polyfil lightly.

Make a slip stitch, fasten off and leave a long tail for sewing.

Attach in front of the big part.

Cute Crochet Garden

FLOWERS

*work with pink yarn (or any color you like!)

1: sc5 into mr = [5]

2: (sc1, ch3, sl in the same st) 5 times

Fasten off and leave a long tail for sewing.

Cute Crochet Garden

Make another flower using the yellow yarn.

Attach them anywhere you'd like!